THANKSGIVING

COOKERY

TRADITIONAL COUNTRY LIFE RECIPES SERIES

THANKSGIVING
COOKERY

James W. Baker
Historian, Plimoth Plantation
Plymouth, Massachusetts

Recipes compiled by
Elizabeth Brabb

*(Editorial Consultant,
Lawrence Farms, NY)*
Vonnie Lawrence

Book Design
Pearl Lau

Consultant
Richard J. Wall, Ph.D.

Cover Illustration
Lisa Adams

The Brick Tower Press ®
1230 Park Avenue, New York, NY 10128
Copyright © 1994, 1998
James W. Baker, Plimoth Plantation
Elizabeth Brabb

Baker, James W. & Brabb, Elizabeth
The Traditional Country Life Recipe Series:
Thanksgiving Cookery — 2nd Edition
Includes Index
ISBN 1-883283-03-5 softcover

Library of Congress Catalog Card
Number: 93-70949
November 1997
Second Edition

"The First Thanksgiving" — Harvest, New Plymouth, 1621

> The Plymouth Pilgrims held a three day harvest celebration in the Fall of 1621, to which they invited the Wampanoag sachem Massasoit. While we may be sure they gave thanks to God for their bounty, it was not a true Thanksgiving in their understanding of the holiday.

THANKSGIVING THEN AND NOW

"The Company makes the Feast"[1]

Thanksgiving Day! What a wealth of images are evoked by this All-American holiday; a multitude of comforting sentiments that would require an American Dickens to do them justice. Valiant be-buckled Pilgrims and their dignified Indian neighbors sit down to dinner in the serenity of an eternal golden autumn afternoon. Radiant white churches welcome cheerful congregations from their rural homesteads supplying the bounty of the harvest. High school and college football teams defend their scholastic honor as preceding generations had under crisp blue autumn skies sensuously spiced with the faint aroma of burning leaves. Generations converge on old New England homesteads where white-haired grandparents welcome the youngest members of the clan. Shocks of corn and heaps of pumpkins dot the fields and fill the barns, and the strutting monarch of the farmyard, the fattened Thanksgiving turkey, marches to his unsuspected fate. Pies are drawn steaming from cast-iron stoves on which bubbling pots foretell the forthcoming feast. All of this would be recognized by generations of Americans as the essence of Thanksgiving.

It is not surprising, therefore, that many people look back nostalgically to the Thanksgivings of their childhood and feel that they would like to recapture the magic, not only for themselves but for their own children. It feels heartless to deny today's children some of the more innocent joys of the past simply because their elders have become bruised and hardened by the world. When we choose to exaggerate the very real tragedies of the past and ignore the accompanying joys and pleasures, we destroy more than our illusions. We break a bond with history and deny our children the strength that traditional societies gain from a commonly shared vision of their heritage.

But our greeting card images, if they ever existed outside of Currier and Ives, are drawn from an American experience largely vanished from our lives. Memories of the holiday as recent as those of Norman Rockwell represent an almost mythical past today. A generation ago American schools and cultural institutions, from the popular press to the prestigious museums, made an effort to find a positive spin on our national myths. Today we live in a disillusioned age that looks at the innocence of these images with an ironic eye. Realists have labored long and hard to exorcise romance and sentiment from our culture, but it was through those channels that the Thanksgiving holiday entered our lives.

Thanksgiving has always worked to re-unite us with our nation's past, to restore community and family ties broken by too great an attention to the daily grind and worries about the future. It is a uniquely ecumenical holiday, which has easily accommodated generations of newcomers to America whatever their faith, politics, or ethnicity. Thanksgiving sentiments have an important role to play, not only in bridging generations but in renewing the cultural ties within our society. We need not forfeit our grasp of life's challenges if we take the time to indulge in some harmless and pleasing Thanksgiving sensibilities. Neither the saccharin images of smiling Pilgrims and cartoon turkeys, the naive pleasure of the old stories nor our personal memories of family dinners and the bittersweet boredom of after-dinner satiety may be objectively accurate but they are part of the cement that holds families — and nations — together.

History of the Holiday in Colonial Times

Since its inception as a Puritan religious observance in colonial New England, Thanksgiving has captured the hearts — and appetites — of the American public — recent immigrants and longtime inhabitants alike. Our Thanksgiving holiday has its origin in the Puritan Thanksgivings of colonial New England. Both the Pilgrims of Plymouth

and the Boston Puritans, who settled New England in the early 17th century, were strict Calvinist Protestants who rejected the religious calendar of holidays that the English people inherited from the Middle Ages. They believed that Christmas, Easter, and the Saints' days were not part of a true Christian church, but later man-made inventions that should be discarded. Instead, they observed only the three religious holidays for which they could find New Testament justification; the Sunday Sabbath, Days of Fasting and Humiliation, and Days of Thanksgiving and Praise.

The Fast Day and the Thanksgiving Day holidays were essentially two sides of the same coin. Thanksgivings marked favorable ("mercies"), and Fast Days unfavorable ("judgements") circumstances in community life. They were declared in response to God's Providence, as the faithful believed that God's pleasure or displeasure with His people was signaled by worldly events. Both were scheduled on this contingency basis and were never assigned fixed positions in the calendar. However, Fast Days more often occurred in the spring (when there was nothing much fresh to eat anyway), while Thanksgivings were usually declared after the harvest in the autumn. Thanksgivings or Fast Days could be declared by individual churches, towns, or the colonial governments at any time. There could be more than one in a single year or none at all. Unlike the Catholic or Anglican Thanksgivings, they were never on Sunday to avoid conflict with the Sabbath. They usually fell on the weekday regularly set aside as "Lecture Day," which was Wednesday in Connecticut and Thursday in Plymouth and Massachusetts Bay. Lecture Day was a mid-week church meeting (often coinciding with the market day) when topical sermons were enjoyed by the colonists.

Despite a number of claims for a chronological "First Thanksgiving" from other parts of the country such as Virginia, Florida, and Texas, the holiday we know today evolved directly from this New England tradition. None of these other claimants contributed to the tradition of regular Thanksgiving observances or influenced the evolution of our modern holiday. Strictly speaking, there never was a "First Thanksgiving" in the sense of a particular celebration that initiated the regular observance of the holiday we know today. The famous 1621 Pilgrim event, which was transformed into "the original" First Thanksgiving in the late 19th century, was in fact not a true Thanksgiving at all. It was rather a secular harvest celebration that as far as we know was never repeated. The first real Calvinist Thanksgiving in New England *was* celebrated in Plymouth Colony, but it was during the summer of 1623 when the colonists declared a Thanksgiving holiday after their crops were saved by a providential shower. The shower had appeared appropriately, and much to the awe of the local Native Americans, after a day of Fasting and Humiliation declared in response to the drought. Following the rain, the grateful colonists declared their first recorded Thanksgiving.

When things were going well, or some special dispensation occurred such as the arrival of a crucial supply ship, a successful harvest, or victory in war, New Englanders declared a day of Thanksgiving. Everyone gathered at the meeting house where they gave thanks to God for their blessings, and then went home to a celebratory dinner that might involve just the family, or be a community event including their friends and neighbors, as well. If things were going badly — there was not enough food to eat, the Native Americans showed signs of resistance, the crops were failing or disease caused a number of unexplained deaths — then a day of Fasting and Humiliation was called for. Again everyone went to church to ask God for His forgiveness and guidance. The people were reminded of their moral and religious responsibilities, and urged to control not only their own sinfulness but also that of other people in the community to avert God's displeasure. There was no big dinner to follow, although a modest meal could be taken in the evening.

The Puritans disputed whether only the unique or impressive acts of Providence could be acknowledged with Thanksgivings, or the "generals" — God's continuing care for His people in providing them with the necessities of life — be celebrated as well. While thanks were given on a regular basis at Sabbath services and in family prayers and graces,

The Pilgrims and the "First Thanksgiving"

A Pilgrim or Puritan Thanksgiving was a holy day marked by sermons and prayers in the morning, which was followed by a generous dinner in the afternoon. There were no games, recreations, or Native American guests.

many people thought it suitable that the community as a whole set some time aside to thank God for these mundane considerations. It was in this spirit that the annually occurring autumn Thanksgiving evolved. Once the harvest was over and the year drawing to a close, the need to bring the community together in some sort of celebratory recognition of the

year's blessings became crucial. In England and the other colonies, the Christmas holiday provided this important social function. In New England, where Christmas had briefly been illegal and not generally celebrated until the mid-19th century, the annual autumn Thanksgiving took over the role Christmas played elsewhere in providing feasting and celebration at the onset of winter.

The custom of annually occurring autumnal Thanksgivings was established throughout New England by the mid-17th century. If Plymouth celebrated the first New England Thanksgiving and, with Boston, established Thursday as the standard day for the event, Connecticut made it an irregular annual holiday. A large part of the pleasurable anticipation associated with Thanksgiving occurred while everyone eagerly waited to hear when it would be scheduled. Once the authorities announced the date a few weeks before the event, each family happily began the process of preparing for the event, baking pies, and arranging with relations for the dinner marking the event. It would be fairest perhaps to say that all of New England shared in the creation of the Thanksgiving holiday.

<u>THANKSGIVING GAINS NATIONAL POPULARITY</u>

In 1777, The Continental Congress declared the first national American Thanksgiving following the providential victory at Saratoga:

November 1, 1777

"Forasmuch as it is the indispensable Duty of all Men to adore the superintending providence of Almighty God; to acknowledge with Gratitude their Obligation to him for benefits received, and to implore such further Blessings as they stand in Need of: And it having pleased him in his abundant Mercy, not only to continue to us the innumerable Bounties of his common providence; but also to smile upon us in the Prosecution of a just and necessary War, for the Defence and Establishment of our inalienable Rights and Liberties…It is therefore recommended to the legislative or executive Powers of these UNITED STATES, to set apart THURSDAY, the eighteenth Day of December

Dinner Among the Puritans and Their Descendants

The standard impression of Thanksgiving in Victorian times was the family dinner. The New England family gathers several generations for games, dances, and dinner on the old homestead.

next, for the Solemn Thanksgiving and Praise: That at one Time and with one voice, the good People may express themselves to the Service of their Divine Benefactor… And it is further recommended, That servile labour, and such Recreations, as, though at other Times innocent, may be unbecoming the Purpose of this Appointment, be omitted on so solemn an Occasion."[2]

The 1777 Thanksgiving proclamation reveals its New England Puritan roots. The day was still officially a religious observance in recognition of God's Providence, and, as on the Sabbath, both work and amusements were forbidden. It does not resemble our idea of a Thanksgiving, with its emphasis on family dinners and popular recreation. Yet beneath these stern sentiments, the old Puritan fervor had declined to the extent that Thanksgiving was beginning to be less of a religious and more of a secular celebration. The focus was shifting from the religious service to the family gathering. Communities still dutifully went to church each Thanksgiving Day, but the social and culinary attractions were increasing in importance.

A contemporary account of a wartime Thanksgiving provides us alternative testimony to the austere official proclamation. Juliana Smith's 1779 Massachusetts' Thanksgiving description, written in a let-

ter to her friend Betsey Smith (and recorded in her diary as well) provides a good example of what the late 18th century celebration meant to the participants. It is so revealing about traditional Thanksgivings with their focus on church, family, food, local charity, giving thanks, and telling stories to warrant being included at length:

"This year it was Uncle Simeon's turn to have the dinner at his house, but of course we all helped them as they help us when it is our turn, & there is always enough for us to do. All the baking of pies & cakes was done at our house & we had the big oven heated & filled twice each day for three days before it was done, & everything was GOOD, though we did have to do without some things that ought to be used. Neither Love nor [paper] Money could buy Raisins, but our good red cherries dried without the pits, did almost as well & happily Uncle Simeon still had some spices in store. The Tables were set in the Dining Hall and even that big room had no space to spare when we were all seated. The Servants had enough ado to get around the Tables & serve us all without over-setting things. There were our two grandmothers side by side. They are always handsome old ladies, but now, many

thought, they were handsomer than ever, & happy they were to look around upon so many of their descendants. Uncle and Aunt Simeon presided at one Table, & Father & Mother at the other. Besides us five boys & girls there were two of the Gales & three Elmers, besides James Browne & Ephraim Cowles. [Five of the last named seven were orphans taught and in all ways provided for by Parson & Mrs. Smith] We had them at our table because they could be best supervised there. Most of the students had gone to their own homes, for the weeks, but Mr. Skiff and Mr. ()— were too far away from their homes. They sat at Uncle Simeon's table & so did Uncle Paul and his family, five of them in all, & Cousins Phin & Poll. Then there were six of the Livingston family next door. They had never seen a Thanksgiving Dinner before, having been used to keep Christmas Day instead, as is the wont in New York and Province. Then there were four Old Ladies who have no longer Homes or Children of their own & so came to us. They were invited by my Mother, but Uncle & Aunt Simeon wished it so."

"Of course we have no Roast Beef. None of us have tasted Beef these three years back as it must all go to the Army, & too little they get, poor fellows. But, Nayquittymaw's Hunters were able to get us a fine red Deer, so that we had a good haunch of Venisson on each Table. These were balanced by huge Chines of Roast Pork at the other ends of the tables. Then there was on one a big Roast Turkey & on the other a Goose, & two big Pigeon pasties. Then there was an abundance of good vegetables of all sorts & one which I do not believe you have seen. Uncle Simeon had imported the Seede from England just before the War began & only this year was there enough for Table use. It is called Sellery & you eat it without cooking. It is very good served with meats. Next year Uncle Simeon says he will be able to raise enough to give us all some. It has to be taken up roots & all & buried in the earth in the cellar through the winter & only pulling up some when you want it to use."

"Our Mince pies were good although we had to use dried Cherries as I told you, & the meat was shoulder of Venisson, instead of beef. The Pumpkin Pies, Apple Tarts & big Indian Puddings lacked for nothing save appetite by the time we got round to them."

"Of course we had no Wine. Uncle Simeon has still a cask or two, but it must be saved for the sick, & indeed, for those who are well, good Cider is a sufficient substitute. There is no Plumb Pudding, but a boiled Suet Pudding, stirred thick with dried Plumbs & Cherries, was called by the old Name and answered to the purpose. All of the other spice had been used in the mince pies, so for this pudding we used a jar of West India preserved Ginger which chanced to be left of the last shipment which Uncle Simeon had from there, we chopped up the Ginger small and stirred it through with the Plumbs and the Cherries. It was extraordinary good. The Day was bitter cold & when we got home from Meeting, which Father did not keep over long by reason of the cold, we were glad eno' of the fire in Uncle's Dining Hall, but by the time the dinner was one-half over those of us who were on the fire side of one Table was forced to get up & carry our plates with us around to the far side of the other Table, while those who had sat there were as glad to bring their plates around to the fire side to get warm. All but the Old Ladies who had a screen put behind their chairs."

"Uncle Simeon was in his best mood, and you know how good that is! He kept both Tables in a roar of laughter with his droll stories of the days when he was studying medicine in Edinborough, & afterwards he & Father & Uncle Paul joined in singing Hymns & Ballads. You know how fine their voices go together. Then we all sang a Hymn and afterwards my dear Father led us in prayer, remembering all Absent Friends before the Throne of Grace, & much I wished *that my dear Betsey was here as one of us, as she has been of yore."*

"We did not rise from the Table until it was quite dark, & then when the dishes had been cleared away we all got round the fire as close as we could, & cracked nuts & sang songs & told stories. At least some told & others listened. You know nobody can exceed the two Grandmothers at telling tales of all the things they have seen themselves, & repeating those of the early years of New England, & even some in the Old England, which they heard in their youth from their Elders. My Father says it is a goodly custom to hand down all worth deeds & traditions from Father to Son, as the Israelites were commanded to do about the Passover & as the Indians here have always done, because the word that is spoken is remembered longer than the one that is written."[3]

National Thanksgivings were proclaimed annually by Congress from 1777 to 1783 which, except for 1782, were all celebrated in December. After a five year hiatus, the practice was revived by President Washington in 1789 and 1795. John Adams declared Thanksgivings in 1798 and 1799, while James Madison declared the holiday twice in 1815; none of these were celebrated in the autumn. After 1815, there were no further national Thanksgivings until the Civil War. As sectional differences widened in the Antebellum period, it was impossible to achieve the consensus to have a national Thanksgiving. The southern states were generally unreceptive to a "Yankee" custom being pressed on them by the federal government. If the federal government neglected the tradition, however, the individual states did not. The New England states continued to declare annual Thanksgivings (usually in November, although not always on the same day), and eventually most of the other states also had independent observations of the holiday. New Englanders were born proselyters and wherever they went during the great westward migration they introduced their favorite holiday. Thanksgiving was adopted first in the Northeast and in the Northwest Territory, then by the middle and western states. At mid-century even the southern states were celebrating their own Thanksgivings.

By the 1840's when the Puritan holy day had largely given way to the Yankee holiday, Thanksgiving was usually depicted in a family setting with dinner as the central event. The original tradition of harvest celebration had weathered Puritan disapproval and quietly reasserted its influence. Newspapers and magazines helped popularize the holiday in its new guise as a secular autumn celebration featuring feasting, family reunions, and charity to the poor. Thanksgiving became an important symbol of the new emphasis on home life and the necessity of enforcing family virtues against the coarse masculine style and cutthroat business practices of the day. This "cult of domesticity" found Thanksgiving a valuable element for promulgating the feminist goals of social reform and the role of the (extended) family as a bastion against the callous workaday world. The holiday focused on the home and hearth where it was hoped a revolution in manners would begin to restore the civilized virtues that had been lost in the new commercial and industrial society.

It is interesting that the same person who was a leading figure in the domesticity movement, Sarah Josepha Hale, also labored for decades to establish Thanksgiving as a national holiday. A New England author and editor of the influential *Godey's Ladies Book*, Hale lobbied for a return to the morality and simplicity of days gone by. Each November from 1846 until 1863 Mrs. Hale printed an editorial urging the federal government to establish Thanksgiving as a national holiday. She was finally gratified when Abraham Lincoln declared the first of our modern series of annual Thanksgiving holidays for the last Thursday in November, 1863. Lincoln had previously declared national Thanksgivings for April, 1862, and again for August 6, 1863, after the northern victory at Gettysburg. The southern states had independently declared Thanksgivings of their own, unsullied by Yankee influences, but would later resent the new national Thanksgiving holiday after the war.

Lincoln went on to declare a similar Thanksgiving observance in 1864, establishing a precedent that was followed by Andrew Johnson in 1865 and by every subsequent president. After a few deviations (December 7, 1865, November 18, 1869), the holiday came to rest on the

last Thursday in November. However, Thanksgiving remained a custom unsanctified by law until 1941! In 1939 Franklin D. Roosevelt departed from tradition by declaring November 23, the next to the last Thursday that year, as Thanksgiving. Considerable controversy (mostly following political lines) arose around this outrage to custom, so that some Americans celebrated Thanksgiving on the 23rd and others on the 30th (including Plymouth, MA). In 1940, the country was once again divided over "Franksgiving" as the Thanksgiving declared for November 21 was called. Thanksgiving was declared for the earlier Thursday again in 1941, but Roosevelt admitted that the earlier date, which had not proven useful to the commercial interests, was a mistake. On November 26, 1941, he signed a bill that established the *fourth* Thursday in November as the national Thanksgiving holiday, which it has been ever since.

<u>The Pilgrims and the "First Thanksgiving"</u>

During the second half of the 19th century, Thanksgiving was more commonly symbolized by its New England origins and its chief dinner constituent, the turkey, than by the Pilgrims' 1621 celebration. In addition to the rural New England theme, there were a diversity of con-

"Thanksgiving in New England Two Hundred Years Ago"
—**Victorian Thanksgiving Fears** *(Frank Leslie's Illustrated 1869: p.180)*

When Victorian illustrators imagined Thanksgiving Day in colonial times, the most common image was one of conflict with the Native Americans. The famous Thanksgiving dinner scenes we are familiar with today became popular after 1900 when the Indian Wars in the West ended.

temporary and historical illustrations and stories, including Thanksgivings on the battlefield, down south with African-Americans, in the urban slums, as well as a few generic colonial New England (and Old England) Puritan images. It is surprising to note that when the colonists are represented, they are less likely to be sharing their feast with their Native American neighbors, than illustrating European and Native American conflict, indicated by a hail of arrows! Apparently the very real dangers of the Indian Wars in the West produced a sense of fear and guilt expressed in this fashion, in graphic contrast with the familiar peaceful autumn pastorals that we associate with the holiday today. It was only after the wars were over that a sentimental regard for the satisfactorily "vanishing Red Man" provoked a national change of heart in which Jennie Brownscombe could create her idyllic "First Thanksgiving" (1914). Even then the image of the Thanksgiving "Pilgrim-Puritan" fleeing a shower of arrows retained a popular appeal.[4]

The association between Thanksgiving and the Pilgrims had been suggested as early as 1841 when Alexander Young identified the 1621 harvest celebration as the "First Thanksgiving" in New England[5] but their importance among the holiday's symbols did not occur until after 1900. It was then that the familiar illustrations of Pilgrims and Native Americans sitting down to dinner in peace and concord appeared widely in calendar art and on patriotic murals. The real New England Thanksgiving, as is shown in the 1777 proclamation, bore less of a resemblance to our modern holiday than the feasting and games of the Pilgrim harvest celebration. But when the Victorians were looking for the historical antecedent of the contemporary Thanksgiving holiday, the Pilgrim festival with its big dinner and charitable hospitality seemed the perfect match. The fact that the 1621 event had not been a Thanksgiving in the Pilgrims' own eyes was irrelevant. The Pilgrim harvest celebration quickly became the mythic "First Thanksgiving" and has remained the primary historical representation of the holiday ever since. The earlier Pilgrim holiday, Forefathers' Day (December 21, the anniversary of the Landing on Plymouth Rock), which had been celebrated since 1769, faded in importance as the Pilgrims increasingly became the patron saints of the American Thanksgiving.

Equally important at the turn of the century was the inspirational image of the Pilgrims and the Native Americans sharing their communal meal in harmony. The country was seriously concerned over immigration and the problems surrounding the integration of new citizens into American culture. The Thanksgiving image of dissimilar ethnic communities co-existing amid peace and plenty was an irresistible symbol. The Pilgrims became the exemplary immigrants whose Protestant virtues made them the preferred model for all later arrivals. Americanization programs, which were intended to socialize the new immigrants by instilling in them the values and beliefs of "real" Americans, made good use of the symbols and ideals of Thanksgiving and the Pilgrims. By 1920, when the Pilgrims' 300th anniversary celebration elevated them to the pinnacle of their fame, their role as Thanksgiving icons and the "spiritual ancestors" of all Americans became permanently fixed in the American psyche.

THANKSGIVING IN OUR OWN TIMES

If there is any element that can be said to dominate the celebration of Thanksgiving, it is the traditional turkey dinner. Most holidays have some sort of culinary associations such as fruit cake and mince pies for Christmas, ham at Easter, or peas and salmon on the Fourth of July, but only Thanksgiving has food as its central feature. Pilgrim images, harvest symbols, church services, and even football take a secondary role to the groaning board. The traditional foods of Thanksgiving, including the turkey and stuffing, onions, potatoes, squash, cranberry sauce, and even the celery have an almost sacramental fixity that marks each family as an orthodox or dissenting party to the holiday tradition. Yet it is equally true that every family has the time honored option of modifying the established menu *just a bit* in line with the family's own vital traditions. There is in truth no single "authentic" Thanksgiving observation, or rather there are innumerable equally valid tributaries that flow into the basic tradition. Every American family, whether they are recent immigrants or descendants of colonial forebears, has its own definition of a "real Thanksgiving" and its appropriate customs. They are all, for their own families, correct.

Thanksgiving is our pre-eminent family holiday. Free from any over-riding religious or even civic agenda, Thanksgiving is the time when Americans are expected to reunite and restore their family ties and recall their own pasts as well as that of the nation. When actual family reunion is not possible, Americans find it proper to honor the Thanksgiving spir-it by gathering together in some public venue and enjoying a common meal that recalls absent relations and Thanksgivings Past with a sacra-mental turkey dinner menu. During wars, in foreign lands, in prisons, in Skid Row missions, in elegant restaurants, or the meanest dive, the appearance of the Thanksgiving bill of fare unites all Americans in a world-wide communion with the national celebration. In the end, we all carry our own Thanksgiving spirit around with us, as Scrooge did with Christmas, and in November we do whatever we need to do to recognize (or reject) its traditional message and meaning.

The problem today, in a time when mobility, divorce, and economic necessity have broken up families and there are fewer and fewer "old homesteads" to return to, is that our ability to honor Thanksgiving as we would truly wish to do so is often wanting. The spirit is willing but the accommodations are weak — or non-existent. This is particularly true for young families on their own and long or distantly separated from their childhood homes and relations. While they may have fond and sentimental memories of past Thanksgivings, or only an unformed longing to participate in the American holiday they have learned about through the media and popular culture, they really have no idea how to begin. They have a general impression of the role of the turkey and the various approved vegetables, but there are no parents or grandparents who can pass down the techniques of how to prepare such an elaborate dinner.

They could just go out to dinner and receive some cardboard turkey over a lump of sawdust stuffing with soupy potato and a dab of gummy cranberry something in a plastic container, but what they want is a real traditional meal. More than just the meal, what they want is their *own* meal, prepared with the same love and understanding that appear in prototypic Norman Rockwell images. But how to begin? What really is a "traditional Thanksgiving dinner"? The standard Thanksgiving meal, despite the numerous Pilgrim images, is not a 17th century but rather a 19th century menu. It reflects the tastes and available foods of that period, especially those that were popular in New England. As we noted earlier, it is equally desirable to substitute dishes from other traditions, as it is the essence of each family's own personal or ethnic heritage that should be

honored in a true Thanksgiving, not just those of Old New England. However, the New England bill of fare remains the foundation of the feast.

While we may imagine that we want to honor the past by having only Real Traditional Pilgrim cooking or whatever, the truth is, what the Pilgrims ate and what we know as a traditional Thanksgiving dinner are quite different things. At the "First Thanksgiving" there were no potatoes, no cranberry sauce, no sweet corn, no apple pies, no gravy, and no celery. There were turkeys, geese, ducks, and roasts of venison, and presumably squash, pumpkin, turnip, and onions (although not creamed). What we really want is the comfort of a living tradition that reflects what we can remember from our childhood. While this evokes the traditions of Victorian times, we are in truth thinking of what our grandparent's generation knew as traditional Thanksgiving cooking. We therefore need not travel further back in time than just before World War II, when the Thanksgivings we remember received their form.

The Thanksgivings between the World Wars were based on the traditions that had evolved in the late 19th century, but there was also then a recognition that some modern "improvements" had crept in, and it was thought correct to try to recapture the simpler menu of yesteryear — just as we are doing today. It is the intention of this book to provide our contemporary audience with the tools needed to prepare their own traditional Thanksgiving dinner; to bridge the years and thus carry the joys of Thanksgivings Past to the rising and future generations. We therefore wish you Happy Thanksgiving and may you have the best of luck in the old holiday traditions.

Footnotes

1- Hyman, Robin, ed. *The Quotation Dictionary*, NY: Collier Books, 1962.

2- Love, W. DeLoss. *Fast and Thanksgiving Days of New England*. Boston: Houghton, Mifflin, 1895, pp. 400-401.

3- Juliana Smith, as quoted in Linton, Ralph and Adelin. *We Gather Together: The Story of Thanksgiving*. New York: Abelard-Schuman, 1949, pp. 73-77.

4- For example, Norman Rockwell's cover for *Life* Magazine ("A Pilgrim's Progress"), Nov. 17, 1921, portrays a Pilgrim boy replete with turkey running from a hail of arrows in the old style. The editor of the Reader's Digest Edition of *Norman Rockwell's America* (New York: Abrams, 1975), Christopher Finch, shows that this image has become quite inexplicable to modern readers when he comments that the scene"...illustrates an aspect of Thanksgiving that does not fall within our present field of experience.") p.142).

5- Young, Alexander. *Chronicles of the Pilgrim Fathers*. Boston: Little, Brown, 1841, p. 231.

A TRADITIONAL
THANKSGIVING FEAST

Turkey

Stuffing

Gravy

Cranberrry Sauce or Jelly

Sweet Potatoes

Potatoes and or Turnips

Onions

Green Vegetables

Chilled Apple Cider

Choice of Dessert

Hot Coffee and Tea

WHOLE ROASTED TURKEY

Roasting a whole turkey:

Preheat oven to 325° F.

(1) Prepare the stuffing a couple of hours in advance to allow it time to cool. Stuff the turkey just before roasting.

(2) Rinse the turkey inside and out with cold water and pat dry.

(3) Season the cavity and the turkey breast with a light sprinkling of salt and pepper.

(4) Stuff the neck loosely; pull the neck skin over stuffing and fasten it with a skewer or poultry pin to the back of the turkey. (see note)

(5) Take the tip ends of the wings and bend them backward so that they are held against the back.

(6) Stuff the body cavity loosely. Close the body with skewers or poultry pins, lacing them with string, or sew it closed with heavy thread. (see note)

(7) Tie the ends of the legs together with a long piece of twine, then bring the twine around the tail, drawing legs close. Tie and cut the twine.

(8) Place the turkey, breast side up, on a wire rack in an uncovered roaster. Brush the skin all over with melted butter. Soak a piece of cheesecloth* in melted butter until evenly coated. Cover top and sides of the turkey with the cheesecloth. Do not add water to the roasting pan.

(9) Roast using the table on the next page as an approximate guide.

(10) Roast uncovered, basting every 30 minutes.

(11) Remove the cheesecloth one half hour before the turkey is done to brown the skin.

(12) When done, remove the skewers and string; place the bird on a hot platter. Set aside 15-20 minutes; then slice and serve. (see page 42 for gravy preparation)

NOTE: Since stuffing expands as it cooks, be sure to pack it loosely.

TEMPERATURE-TIME TABLE		
Weight	Time	Serves
8-12 lbs.	2 3/4-3 3/4 hrs	10
12-16 lbs.	3 3/4-4 3/4 hrs	14
16-20 lbs.	4 3/4-5 3/4 hrs	18
20-24 lbs.	5 1/4-6 1/4 hrs	22

✸ INGREDIENTS

stuffing (optional)
1 turkey
salt
pepper
3 skewers or poultry pins
1/2 cup of melted butter
1 piece of cheesecloth, 3 feet long
twine

*The original Fannie Farmer recipe, in 1896, describes the following technique instead of using cheesecloth. This works, but the turkey won't brown as well on the outside. Blend butter and flour. With your hands, massage the roux mixture into the turkey skin for several minutes; then set aside for an hour outside the oven. Roast the turkey in a 325° F. pre-heated oven for 35 minutes. Reduce heat but continue baking, basting occasionally with melted butter for an hour and a half depending on the size of the turkey. (see the Temperature-Time Table)

ROASTED TURKEY BREAST

Preheat the oven to 325° F.

(1) Rinse the turkey with cold water and pat dry.
(2) Season the turkey with a light sprinkling of salt and pepper.
(3) Place turkey, cut side down, on a rack in an uncovered roaster.
(4) Brush turkey with melted butter. Soak a piece of cheesecloth in melted butter and use to cover the top and sides of the turkey.
(5) Roast uncovered, using the following table as an approximate guide, basting every 30 minutes.
(6) Meanwhile, prepare the stuffing.
(7) When half done, remove the turkey to a platter. Cut a double thickness of heavy brown or white paper in an oval about the size of the turkey. Grease well. Place on the rack in the roaster, and arrange the stuffing, mounded, on it. Any excess stuffing should be put in a covered baking dish and baked with the turkey during the last 1/2 hour.
(8) Place the bird skin side up, over the stuffing. Return to the oven and

⚜ INGREDIENTS

turkey breast
salt
pepper
1/2 cup of melted butter
1 piece of cheesecloth, 3 feet long
stuffing (optional)

TEMPERATURE-TIME TABLE		
Weight	Time	Serves
5-8 lbs. ....1 1/2-2 hrs....................7		
8-10 lbs. ....2-2 1/2 hrs....................9		
10-12 lbs. ....2 1/2-3 hrs...................11		

complete the roasting. Baste to moisten the cheesecloth.
(9) Remove the cheesecloth one half hour before the turkey is done to brown the skin.
(10) When done place the turkey, on a platter. Spoon the stuffing into a serving dish. Set aside for 15-20 minutes; then slice and serve. (see page 42 for gravy preparation)

BREAD STUFFING

(1) Place the butter and water in a deep kettle and heat until the butter has melted.
(2) Add the onion, celery, poultry seasoning, parsley, salt and pepper and simmer until the vegetables are tender.
(3) Add the bread crumbs and heat well, without browning, stirring frequently.
(4) Cool the stuffing completely.
(5) Stuff the turkey just before roasting.
(6) Leftover stuffing can be baked in a covered baking dish in the oven with the turkey during the last half hour of roasting.

Giblet Stuffing: add cooked giblets, which have been coarsely chopped.

Corn Bread Stuffing: substitute corn bread crumbs for the regular bread crumbs.

INGREDIENTS

1/2 cup of butter
1/2 cup of water
1 cup of minced onion
1/2 cup of diced celery
1 1/2 teaspoons of poultry seasoning (optional)
1/2 cup of minced parsley
salt and pepper to taste
10 cups of lightly-packed bread crumbs or cubes from day-old bread

STUFFS THE NECK AND-BODY CAVITIES OF A 10-POUND TURKEY

POTATO-MEAT STUFFING

(1) Boil the potatoes in enough water to cover until done, approximately 25-30 minutes
(2) Meanwhile, sauté the ground beef, ground pork, onion, and celery in a large skillet over medium heat until well done.
(3) Drain all the rendered fat from the meat.
(4) Add the poultry seasoning, salt, and pepper to the meat mixture and blend well.
(5) When the potatoes are done, drain and mash them well, adding just enough milk so that they are smooth but still fairly stiff (they will thin somewhat when they are baked in the turkey). Do not add butter; the meat will supply the needed richness.
(6) Add the meat mixture to the potatoes and blend well.
(7) Cool the stuffing completely.
(8) Stuff the turkey just before roasting.
(9) Leftover stuffing can be baked in a covered baking dish in the oven with the turkey during the last half hour of roasting.

❀ INGREDIENTS

15-17 russet potatoes, washed, peeled, and quartered
3 pounds of lean ground beef
2 pounds of lean ground pork
1 cup of minced onion
1 cup of minced celery
1 1/2-2 cups of milk
2 tablespoons of poultry season- ing, or to taste
salt and pepper to taste

NOTE: This recipe is easily halved for a 10-12 pound turkey.

STUFFS A BIG TURKEY
22-24 POUNDS, NECK
AND BODY CAVITIES

CELERY STUFFING

(1) Place water and butter in a deep kettle and heat until the butter has melted.
(2) Add the celery, onions, poultry seasoning, salt and pepper to the boiling water.
(3) Cover and cook until the onions are tender.
(4) Add the bread crumbs and mix thoroughly with a fork.
(5) Cool the stuffing completely.
(6) Stuff the turkey just before roasting.
(7) Leftover stuffing can be baked in a covered baking dish in the oven with the turkey during the last half hour of roasting.

✹ INGREDIENTS

1 cup of boiling water
1 cup of butter
4 cups of finely diced celery
1 cup of minced onion
2 teaspoons of poultry seasoning (optional)
16 cups of lightly-packed day-old bread crumbs
salt and pepper to taste

STUFFS NECK AND BODY CAVITIES OF A 10-POUND TURKEY

CHESTNUT STUFFING

Preheat oven to 500° F.

(1) Wash chestnuts and make a long slit through the shell on both sides of each chestnut. Bake for 15 minutes. Remove from oven and peel off the shells and skins.

(2) Boil the chestnuts for 20 minutes in enough salted water to cover. Drain the chestnuts and then chop medium fine; set aside.

(3) Melt the butter in a skillet and sauté the sausage meat and onion until the sausage is cooked and the onion is tender, approximately 5 minutes. Set aside.

(4) Add the chicken stock, sage, parsley, salt, and pepper to the bread crumbs.

(5) Combine the 3 mixtures.

(6) Cool the stuffing completely.

(7) Stuff the turkey just before roasting.

(8) Leftover stuffing can be baked in a covered baking dish in the oven with the turkey during the last half hour of roasting.

✸ INGREDIENTS

1/2 pound of chestnuts
1/4 cup of butter
1/2 pound of sausage meat
1/2 cup of minced onion
1/2 cup of hot chicken stock
2 teaspoons of dried sage
1 tablespoon of minced parsley
4 cups of lightly-packed crumbs
 from toasted bread
salt and pepper to taste
2 tablespoons of sherry
 (optional)

NOTE: Sherry enhances the flavor of this recipe.

STUFFS THE NECK CAVITY OF AN 8-POUND TURKEY

CORN STUFFING

(1) Bring the water to a boil and cook celery, covered, until tender, for approximately 15-20 minutes. Drain and set aside.
(2) Sauté the onion in butter until transparent.
(3) Combine the celery, onion mixture, sage, parsley, bread crumbs, corn, salt, and pepper.
(4) Mix well with a fork.
(5) Cool the stuffing completely.
(6) Stuff the turkey just before r oasting.
(7) Leftover stuffing can be baked in a covered baking dish in the oven with the turkey during the last half hour of roasting.

❁ INGREDIENTS

2 cups of water
3 cups of diced celery
2/3 cup of minced onion
1 cup of butter
1 teaspoon of dried sage
1/4 cup of minced parsley
8 cups of lightly-packed day-old bread crumbs
4 cups of whole kernel corn
salt and pepper to taste

STUFFS THE NECK AND-BODY CAVITIES OF AN 8-POUND TURKEY

MOIST BREAD STUFFING

(1) Bring the water to a boil.
(2) Add the butter, celery, and onion to the boiling water and simmer for 5 minutes.
(3) Add the poultry seasoning, parsley, mustard, bread crumbs, salt, and pepper and mix well with a fork.
(4) Cool the stuffing completely.
(5) Stuff the turkey just before roasting.
(6) Leftover stuffing can be baked in a covered baking dish in the oven with the turkey during the last half hour of roasting.

❁ INGREDIENTS

1 1/2 cups of water
1/2 cup of butter
1/2 cup of diced celery
1 1/2 cups of minced onion
1 teaspoon of poultry seasoning (optional)
1/2 cup of minced parsley
2 teaspoons of dry mustard
12 cups of lightly-packed day-old bread crumbs
salt and pepper to taste

STUFFS THE BODY CAVITY OF AN 8-POUND TURKEY

SAUSAGE STUFFING

(1) Cook the sausage meat, celery, and onion together in a skillet over medium heat until the sausage meat is cooked, approximately 10 minutes.
(2) Drain the rendered fat and turn the mixture into a large bowl.
(3) Add the butter, bread crumbs, parsley, and sage and stir with a fork to combine.
(4) Cool the stuffing completely.
(5) Stuff the turkey just before roasting.
(6) Leftover stuffing can be baked in a covered baking dish in the oven with the turkey during the last half hour of roasting.

✸ INGREDIENTS

1 pound of sausage meat
1/2 cup of diced celery
1 cup of minced onion
1/2 cup of butter, melted
8 cups of lightly-packed day-old bread crumbs
1/4 cup of minced parsley
1/2 teaspoon of dried sage

STUFFS THE BODY CAVITY
OF AN 8-POUND TURKEY

APPLE STUFFING

(1) In a saucepan mix together the butter, milk, celery, onion, salt, marjoram, cinnamon and pepper; cook over low heat until the vegetables are tender.
(2) Blend the bread cubes, and apples.
(3) Lightly toss the seasoned, melted butter with the bread mixture.
(4) Cool the stuffing completely.
(5) Stuff the turkey just before roasting.
(6) Leftover stuffing can be baked in a covered baking dish in the oven with the turkey during the last half hour of roasting.

❊ INGREDIENTS

3/4 cup of butter, melted
3/4 cup of milk
1/3 cup of chopped celery with leaves
1 cup of chopped onion
salt to taste
1/2 teaspoon of marjoram
1/2 teaspoon of ground cinnamon
1/4 teaspoon of ground black pepper
8 cups of soft bread cubes
2 cups of washed, quartered, pared, and diced apples

STUFFS THE NECK AND BODY CAVITIES OF A 10-POUND TURKEY

OYSTER STUFFING

(1) In a saucepan mix together the butter, milk, celery, onion, thyme, salt, and pepper; cook over low heat until the vegetables are tender.
(2) Blend the bread cubes, and oysters.
(3) Lightly toss the seasoned, melted butter into the bread mixture
(4) Cool the stuffing completely.
(5) Stuff the turkey just before roasting.
(6) Leftover stuffing can be baked in a covered baking dish in the oven with the turkey during the last half hour of roasting.

❀ INGREDIENTS

3/4 cup of butter, melted
3/4 cup of milk
1/3 cup of chopped celery with leaves
1 cup of chopped onion
1/2 teaspoon of thyme
salt to taste
1/4 teaspoon of ground black pepper
8 cups of soft bread cubes
1 pint of oysters, drained and minced

STUFFS THE NECK AND BODY CAVITIES OF A 10-POUND TURKEY

VELVETY BROWN GRAVY

(1) When the turkey is done, place on a platter and cover loosely with foil.

(2) Pour the drippings from the roasting pan into a 2-cup measuring cup. Reserve 1/4 cup of this liquid.

(3) Pour reserved liquid and 1 cup of water into the roasting pan and, over medium heat, stir and scrape the dark bits stuck to the pan; these will lightly brown the liquid.

(4) Whisk the flour into the roasting pan mixture until well blended.

(5) Gradually add the remaining cup of liquid to the roasting pan, stirring constantly.

(6) Continue to heat over a low flame until the gravy boils and thickens to velvety smoothness.

(7) Season with salt and pepper to taste.

To cook giblets: Clean and remove fat from the giblets. Place the neck, heart, and gizzard in a saucepan with 1 stalk of celery chopped with its leaves, 2 peppercorns, 1/2 bay leaf, and 1 sliced small onion, in cold water to cover. Simmer, covered, for 2 hours. Add the liver and 1/2 teaspoon of salt for the last 15 minutes. When done, drain (saving the liquid for other uses), discard the vegetables, and chop the giblets coarsely.

NOTE: *If a thinner gravy is desired, add more water. A little sherry, burgundy, chutney, or a pinch of herbs may also be added.*

Rich Brown Gravy: Substitute milk, or milk and cream, for part of the water. Or, to thicken gravy, add 1/3 cup of sour cream (being careful not to let the gravy boil).

Chestnut Gravy: To 2 cups of gravy, add 1/2 cup of chestnuts, shelled and cooked as in Chestnut Stuffing (page 36), then chopped fine.

Cranberry Gravy: To 2 cups of gravy, add 1/2 cup of jellied cranberry sauce, beaten smooth with a whisk.

Mushroom Gravy: To 2 cups of gravy, add 1/4 pound of sliced, washed mushrooms which have been cooked in drippings in a saucepan until tender, about 5 minutes.

Giblet Gravy: To 2 cups of gravy, add the chopped cooked giblets from the turkey.

✿ INGREDIENTS

1/4 cup of drippings from the bird
4 tablespoons of flour
2 cups of warm water or giblet cooking water
salt and pepper to taste

MAKES 2 CUPS

CRANBERRY JELLY

(1) Pick over and wash the cranberries.
(2) Bring the water to a boil.
(3) Add the berries to the boiling water.
(4) Boil until all berries burst, approximately 10 minutes.
(5) Pour the berries into a sieve lined with cheesecloth and suspend over a bowl.
(6) Let the cranberry juice drip undisturbed for at least 1 hour.
(7) Return the juice to the saucepan and add the sugar.
(8) Bring the mixture to a full rolling boil slowly, stirring constantly until all the sugar has dissolved.
(9) Continue to boil for about 5 minutes or until the mixture falls in a sheet from the spoon.
(10) Pour at once into a wet mold, or sterilized glasses.
(11) Chill for several hours until set; unmold when ready to serve.

✸ INGREDIENTS

4 cups of cranberries
1 piece of cheesecloth
1 cup of water
2 cups of granulated sugar

NOTE: This recipe can be made a couple of days in advance.

SERVES 6

BLANCHE'S
CRANBERRY SAUCE

(1) Pick over and wash the cranberries.
(2) Bring the water to a boil in a 4-quart saucepan.
(3) Add the cranberries and sugar to the boiling water and blend well.
(4) Simmer for 5 minutes, stirring occasionally.
(5) Remove from the heat and let cool to room temperature.
(6) Pour the cranberry mixture into a serving bowl and add the mandarin oranges without the syrup.
(7) Chill overnight before serving.

❁ INGREDIENTS

2 cups of water
4 cups of cranberries
3 cups of granulated sugar
11 ounces of mandarin oranges in a light sauce

MAKES 4 CUPS

EASY CRANBERRY SAUCE

(1) Pick over and wash the cranberries.
(2) Put the sugar and water into a saucepan and bring the mixture slowly to a boil, stirring constantly.
(3) Boil 10 minutes, or until a thin syrup forms.
(4) Add the cranberries and simmer gently until the some of the berries have burst.
(5) Empty into a serving bowl and chill well before serving.

❋ INGREDIENTS

4 cups of cranberries
1 3/4 cups of granulated sugar
2 cups of water

MAKES 4 CUPS

SPICY CRANBERRY SAUCE

(1) Place the cinnamon, cloves, and allspice into a piece of cheese cloth and tie up into a bag.
(2) Combine the sugar, water, salt, and spice bag in a saucepan and stir over low heat until the sugar is dissolved. Bring to a boil and boil uncovered for 5 minutes.
(3) Add the cranberries and continue to boil uncovered, without stirring, until the berries pop open.
(4) Remove the spice bag and pour the sauce into a serving bowl.
(5) Chill for several hours before serving.

❀ INGREDIENTS

1 3-inch piece of stick cinnamon
2 whole cloves
2 allspice berries
1 piece of cheese cloth
1 cup of sugar
1 cup of water
1/8 teaspoon of salt
2 cups (1/2 pound) of cranberries, washed and sorted

MAKES 2 CUPS

47

RAW CRANBERRY AND APPLE RELISH

(1) Pick over and wash the cranberries.
(2) Chop the cranberries and the apple coarsely using a food chopper or a food processor. Empty into a large bowl.
(3) Finely grate the orange and lemon zest; then remove the remaining pith.
(4) Add the zest to the cranberry and apple mixture.
(5) Quarter the orange and lemon and discard the seeds. Chop the orange and lemon coarsely.
(6) Combine the two mixtures.
(7) Add the sugar and blend well.
(8) Chill for several hours before serving.

✱ INGREDIENTS

2 cups of cranberries
1 tart apple, pared and cored
1 small orange
1/2 lemon
1 cup of granulated sugar

MAKES 3 CUPS

RAW CRANBERRY AND ORANGE RELISH

(1) Pick over and wash the cranberries.
(2) Chop the cranberries coarsely using a food chopper or a food processor. Empty into a large bowl and set aside.
(3) Finely grate the orange zest; then remove the remaining pith. Add the zest to the cranberries.
(4) Slice the oranges in half and remove the seeds; process it coarsely and add to the cranberries.
(5) Add the sugar and allspice and mix well.
(6) Chill for several hours before serving.

❀ INGREDIENTS

2 cups of cranberries
2 small oranges
3/4 cup of granulated sugar
1/4 teaspoon of ground allspice

MAKES 2 CUPS

CANDIED SWEET POTATOES

(1) Boil the well-scrubbed sweet potatoes in enough water to cover for 25-35 minutes, or until tender when pierced with a fork. Drain. To dry the potatoes, shake the pan over low heat.
(2) Peel the sweet potatoes and set them aside.
(3) In a large, heavy skillet, melt the butter.
(4) Add the sugar and salt; heat until the mixture bubbles.
Add the sweet potatoes.
(5) Cook over medium heat for approximately 20 minutes or until the sweet potatoes are well-glazed. Turn the sweet potatoes several times.

❀ INGREDIENTS

6 medium sweet potatoes
  or yams
1/2 cup of butter
1/2 cup of brown sugar, light
  or dark, firmly packed
1/4 teaspoon of salt

SERVES 4-6

CANDIED SWEET POTATOES
DELUXE

Preheat oven to 375° F.

(1) Boil the well-scrubbed sweet potatoes in enough lightly salted water to cover for approximately 30-35 minutes.

(2) Peel and cut sweet potatoes into halves lengthwise.

(3) Arrange the sweet potatoes in a large buttered baking dish.

(4) In a saucepan, combine the brown sugar, butter, milk, nutmeg, cinnamon, salt, and pepper and boil for 5 minutes.

(5) Pour the syrup over the sweet potatoes.

(6) Top with the nuts.

(7) Bake for 30 minutes, basting occasionally.

Skillet Preparation: Arrange the cooked, halved sweet potatoes in a large skillet. Pour the syrup over the potatoes and simmer for 20 minutes, turning and basting occasionally. Top with the nuts.

❀ INGREDIENTS

6 medium sweet potatoes
1 cup of brown sugar, light or dark, firmly packed
1/2 cup of butter
1/4 cup of milk
1/4 teaspoon of ground nutmeg
1/4 teaspoon of ground cinnamon
salt and pepper to taste
1/2 cup of coarsely chopped pecans (optional)

NOTE: This dish can alternatively be topped with more brown sugar, shredded coconut, or maple sugar.

SERVES 6

SWEET POTATO ROYALE

Preheat the oven to 350° F.

(1) Boil the well-scrubbed sweet potatoes in enough lightly salted water to cover for approximately 30-35 minutes. Drain.

(2) To dry the potatoes, shake the pan over low heat. Peel the potatoes.

(3) In a bowl, mash the potatoes thoroughly using a potato masher, food mill, or ricer.

(4) Gradually whip in the butter, milk, nutmeg, salt, and pepper until the potatoes are fluffy.

(5) Add the coconut and mix well.

(6) Spoon the mixture into a large buttered baking dish; bake for 20 minutes.

(7) Cut the marshmallows in half.

(8) Remove the baking dish from the oven and arrange the marshmallow halves around the top. Return the baking dish to the oven and bake for 5-10 minutes longer, or until the marshmallows are lightly browned and partially melted.

✺ INGREDIENTS

6 medium sweet potatoes
4 tablespoons of butter
1/2 cup of warm milk or half and half
1/4 teaspoon of nutmeg
salt and pepper to taste
1/3 cup of shredded coconut
12 marshmallows

SERVES 6

MASHED POTATOES

(1) Boil the potatoes in enough cold water to cover, for 35-40 minutes, or until tender.
(2) Drain the potatoes.
(3) Mash thoroughly, using a potato masher or a food ricer.
(4) Gradually add enough butter and milk to make the potatoes fluffy and creamy.
(5) Season with salt and white pepper to taste.

❂ INGREDIENTS

10 medium russet potatoes, peeled and quartered
6 tablespoons of butter
3/4 cup of warm milk
salt and white pepper to taste

SERVES 7-8

MASHED POTATOES
WITH GARLIC

(1) Boil the potatoes and garlic in enough cold water to cover, for 35-40 minutes, or until tender.
(2) Drain the potatoes and garlic reserving 1/4 cup of the liquid.
(3) Mash thoroughly, using a potato masher or a food ricer.
(4) Gradually add enough butter, milk, and reserved liquid to make the potatoes fluffy and creamy.
(5) Season with salt and white pepper to taste.

✹ INGREDIENTS

10 medium russet potatoes, peeled and quartered
3 large cloves of garlic, peeled and quartered
6 tablespoons of butter
1/2 cup of warm milk
salt and white pepper to taste

SERVES 7-8

MASHED TURNIPS AND POTATOES

(1) Scrub, pare, and cut turnip into 2-inch cubes.
(2) Place turnips, salt, and sugar in a saucepan with enough boiling water to cover.
(3) Boil for 35-40 minutes, or until tender.
(4) Drain thoroughly.
(5) Mash the turnips with a potato masher adding butter, parsley, salt and white pepper to taste, while you mash.
(6) Continue to mash with a hand held mixer, if necessary, until the turnips are smooth.
(7) Combine 1 1/2 cups of mashed turnip with the hot mashed potatoes. Correct seasonings if necessary.

✹ INGREDIENTS

1 1/2 pounds of turnip (white or yellow)
1 teaspoon of salt (optional)
1 teaspoon of sugar
4 tablespoons of butter
2 teaspoons of minced parsley
white pepper and salt to taste
4 cups of mashed potatoes (page 53)

SERVES 4-6

YELLOW TURNIPS
(RUTABAGAS)

(1) Scrub the turnips well, pare, and cut into 2-inch cubes.
(2) Place the turnips, salt, and sugar with enough boiling water to cover in a saucepan.
(3) Boil for 35-40 minutes, or until tender. Drain thoroughly.
(4) Season the turnips with lemon juice, butter, parsley, salt and pepper to taste.

Mashed Yellow Turnips: prepare as above, then mash them well with a potato masher then hand held mixer until smooth.

✹ INGREDIENTS

2 pounds of yellow turnips
1 teaspoon of salt (optional)
1 teaspoon of sugar
1 teaspoon of lemon juice
6 tablespoons of butter, melted
1 teaspoon minced parsley
salt and pepper to taste

NOTE: Buy heavy, firm, yellow turnips. Those light in weight may be woody, pithy, and strong-flavored.

SERVES 4

WHITE TURNIPS

(1) Remove the turnip tops.
(2) Scrub turnips; pare and cut into thin slices.
(3) Boil turnips in enough water to cover, with salt and sugar.
(4) Boil for 25-30 minutes, or until tender. Drain well.
(5) Season with butter, lemon juice, salt and white pepper to taste, and sprinkle with minced parsley or paprika.

Mashed White Turnips: prepare as above, then mash them well with a potato masher before adding the seasonings.

❋ INGREDIENTS

2 pounds of white turnips
1 teaspoon of salt
1/2 teaspoon of sugar
6 tablespoons of butter
1 teaspoon of lemon juice
salt and white pepper to taste
1 1/2 teaspoons of minced parsley, or paprika

NOTE: *White turnip tops, if attached, should be fresh, green, and young; the turnips should be firm and heavy; avoid those light in weight for their size, as they may be woody, pithy, and strong in flavor.*

SERVES 4

CREAMED ONIONS

(1) Blanch the onions in boiling water for 1-2 minutes and then peel off the first layer of skin.

(2) In a medium size saucepan, bring approximately 1 inch of lightly salted water to a boil.

(3) Add the onions and cook until they are tender, approximately 20-25 minutes (Overcooking develops a strong flavor.) Drain.

(4) Partially fill the base of a double boiler with water. Set the top in place, cover, and bring to a boil.

(5) Melt the butter in the top of the double boiler, then whisk in the flour and nutmeg until it forms a thick paste.

(6) Gradually add the milk, whisking constantly to avoid lumps.

(7) Remove from heat when the sauce is thick and smooth. Add the onions and stir gently to avoid breaking up the onions.

(8) Season to taste with salt, and pepper.

✸ INGREDIENTS

1 1/2 pounds of white onions
2 tablespoons of butter
2 1/4 tablespoons of flour
a pinch of nutmeg
1 1/2 cups of milk or
  half-and-half
a pinch of salt
a pinch of pepper

NOTE: *A bit of sherry may be added with the milk for a slightly different taste.*

SERVES 4

BUTTERED ONIONS

(1) Follow the first three steps on the adjacent page for Creamed Onions.
(2) Season with salt, white pepper, and butter. Stir gently to avoid breaking up the onions.

Glazed Onions: After the onions have been cooked until tender, blend 2 tablespoons of butter, 6 tablespoons of granulated sugar, and 2 teaspoons of water in a large skillet over low heat. Add onions; cook until golden and glazed, turning often to avoid sticking and burning.

❀ INGREDIENTS

1 1/2 pounds of white onions
salt and white pepper to taste
6 tablespoons of butter

NOTE: Adding 1/4 cup of thin cream makes this dish a little creamier.

SERVES 4

STUFFED CELERY

(1) Wash the celery and trim off the bottom of the bunch.
(2) Remove as many strings as possible.
(3) Cut each stalk horizontally into 3 pieces; trim off some of the leaves.
(4) Blend the cream cheese, blue cheese, and nuts.
(5) With a spatula or butter knife scoop the cheese mixture into the celery troughs. Sprinkle the stuffed stalks with paprika.
(6) Keep well chilled until served.

❀ INGREDIENTS

1 bunch of celery
8-ounces of cream cheese, softened
8-ounces of blue cheese, softened
1/3 cup of chopped walnuts or pecans, (optional)
paprika

SERVES 8

GREEN BEANS

(1) Wash the beans and remove the ends and strings.
(2) Cut the beans (see below).
(3) Add the beans to enough lightly salted boiling water to cover.
(4) Boil until tender-crisp.
(5) Season to taste with butter, salt, and pepper.

Snapped beans: cut or snap into 2-inch pieces; cook for 5-10 minutes.

Cross-cut beans: cut into thin, slanted, crosswise slices; cook for 5-10 minutes.

French-cut beans: cut into thin, lengthwise strips; cook for 2-5 minutes.

❀ INGREDIENTS

1 1/2 pounds of green beans
butter to taste
salt and pepper to taste

SERVES 4

Buttered Green Beans: Drain the beans, saving liquid. Boil this liquid down to a few tablespoons. Add to the beans with salt and pepper and butter to taste.

Garlic Green Beans: Sauté 1 peeled and minced clove of garlic in 1/4 cup of butter until tender and toss with the hot green beans.

Green Bean Medley: Combine the hot green beans with 1/4 cup of hot whole kernel corn, 1/4 cup of hot diced celery, 8 hot small onions, 1/4 cup of hot green limas, 1/4 cup of hot peas, and 1/4 cup of hot mushrooms. Season to taste with salt, pepper, and butter.

Herb Buttered Green Beans: Toss 1/4 cup of melted butter, 1 teaspoon of lemon juice, and 1 teaspoon of dried rosemary, tarragon, or basil with the hot beans.

GREEN BEANS
with MUSHROOMS

(1) Wash and remove the ends and strings of the beans.
(2) Cut the beans into 2-inch pieces.
(3) Wash and slice the mushrooms.
(4) Combine the onion, milk, and butter in a medium saucepan; heat over low heat until butter is melted, stirring constantly.
(5) Add the mushrooms to the milk mixture and blend well.
(6) Cover and cook over low heat until tender, for about 20 minutes.
(7) Add the beans to the mixture and continue to cook over low heat for 5 minutes or until the beans are tender-crisp.
(8) Add the cream, salt and pepper.
(9) Simmer until cream is warm. Serve.

❈ INGREDIENTS

2 pounds of green beans
1/2 pound of fresh mushrooms
1 cup of minced onion
1/2 cup of milk
4 tablespoons of butter
1/2 cup of light cream
salt and pepper to taste

SERVES 6-8

GREEN BEANS IN AN HERB SAUCE

(1) Wash and remove the ends and strings of the beans.
(2) Add the beans to enough lightly salted boiling water to cover.
(3) Boil for 5 minutes, or until just tender. Drain and set aside.
(4) Meanwhile, melt the butter in a medium saucepan; add onions, garlic, and celery. Sauté until the onions are translucent, stirring occasionally.
(5) Add the parsley and rosemary.
(6) Simmer for 8 minutes.
(7) Toss well with the drained, cooked beans.

❋ INGREDIENTS

1 1/2 pounds of green beans
1/4 cup butter
3/4 cup of minced onion
1 clove of garlic, minced
1/4 cup of minced celery
1/4 cup of minced parsley
1/4 teaspoon of dried rosemary
salt and pepper to taste

SERVES 4

BUTTERED GREENS

(1) Choose one green from the table.

(2) Cut off and discard root ends, tough stems, and yellowed leaves before washing. With kale, cut out and discard midribs.

(3) Wash at least 3 times in warm water, lifting out each leaf from the water and shaking well, so that sand sinks to the bottom of the sink.

(4) Place in a large pot with the water still clinging to the leaves after washing. (If leaves are old or tough such as kale, add 1/2 inch of boiling water.)

(5) Add 1/2 teaspoon of salt for each pound of greens. The onion may be added if desired.

(6) Cover and simmer until just tender-crisp (see time table at right), tossing occasionally with a fork. Drain well.

(7) If desired, slash through cooked greens with kitchen shears or two knives several times.

(8) Season with salt, pepper, nutmeg, and butter.

❂ INGREDIENTS

1 pound of greens (see below):
1/2 teaspoon of salt
1/2 a small onion, thinly sliced (optional)
salt and pepper, to taste
a pinch of nutmeg (optional)
butter to taste.

COOKING-TIME TABLE	
Greens	Minutes
beet tops	5-15
chicory	4-10
collard greens	10-15
dandelion greens	10-20
escarole	10-12
kale	10-15
mustard greens	7-10
spinach	6-10
swiss chard	3-10
turnip greens	8-15

1 POUND SERVES 4

HOT APPLE CIDER

(1) Place the spices in the cheesecloth and tie up into a small bag.
(2) Pour apple cider into a medium saucepan.
(3) Add spice bag and simmer for 15 minutes.
(4) Remove spice bag.
(5) Serve immediately.

✸ INGREDIENTS

1 stick of cinnamon
4 whole cloves
4 whole allspice
1 small piece of cheesecloth
1 quart of apple cider

SERVES 4

DOUBLE CRUST PASTRY

(1) Sift the flour and salt into a medium mixing bowl.
(2) Cut the shortening into the flour using a pastry blender, two knives, or your fingers until the mixture resembles a course meal.
(3) Sprinkle water onto the flour mixture, a little at a time, stirring with a fork until the particles stick together when pressed gently with the fork.
(4) Form the pastry into a ball and place it in a bowl and cover with plastic wrap. Chill for 1/2 hour before using.
(5) Roll out pastry as directed in your recipe.

✿ INGREDIENTS

2 1/4 cups of all-purpose flour
1 teaspoon of salt
3/4 cup of shortening
4 to 6 tablespoons of ice cold water

NOTE: *If using your fingers to cut the shortening into the flour, do so quickly so that the heat from your fingers does not melt the shortening.*

MAKES ONE DOUBLE-CRUST PIE, OR TWO SINGLE-CRUST PIES

CRANBERRY APPLE PIE

Preheat oven to 425° F.

(1) Line a 9-inch pie plate with pastry; prick the dough all over with a fork. Chill.
(2) Mix the sugar, flour, cinnamon, salt, and water in a large saucepan and heat until the sugar dissolves.
(3) Pick over and wash the berries.
(4) Slowly add the berries to the sugar mixture and simmer until their skins begin to pop.
(5) Add the lemon rind and butter; mix lightly with a fork. Cool this mixture slightly.
(6) Pare, quarter, core, and thinly slice the apples.
(7) Place 1/2 of the apples in the pastry lined pie plate.
(8) Cover the apples with 1/2 of the berry mixture.
(9) Top with the remaining apples and the remaining berry mixture.
(10) Roll out the top crust and cut at least two vents to permit steam to escape while baking.
(11) Place the top crust on the pie; trim it and seal it by moistening

❀ INGREDIENTS

1 Double Crust Pastry (page 66)
1 1/4 cups of granulated sugar
2 tablespoons of all-purpose flour
1/4 teaspoon of ground cinnamon
1/4 teaspoon of salt
1/3 cup of water
2 cups of fresh cranberries
1 1/2 teaspoons of grated lemon rind
2 tablespoons of butter, melted
2 cups of tart apples

---

the edge of the bottom crust with milk and pressing the top crust down with the tines of a dinner fork or flute the edge with your fingers.
(12) Bake on the bottom rack for 30-40 minutes, or until the pastry is a light golden brown.
(13) Cool on a wire rack.

SERVES 6

CRANBERRY LATTICE PIE

Preheat the oven to 450° F.

(1) Line a 9-inch pie plate with half of the pastry; prick the dough all over with a fork and chill.

(2) In a medium-size saucepan mix together the sugar, cinnamon, orange juice, and water.

(3) Stir this mixture over medium heat until the sugar is dissolved then increase the heat and bring the mixture to a boil.

(4) Pick over and wash the berries.

(5) Add the cranberries and cook slowly for 3-4 minutes or until the skins of the berries start to pop.

(6) Blend the corn starch and cold water into a smooth paste.

(7) Add a small amount of the cranberry mixture to the cornstarch paste and blend well.

(8) Blend the cornstarch mixture with the hot cranberries, stirring constantly.

(9) Bring this mixture rapidly to a boil and cook for 3 minutes, stirring constantly. Remove from heat.

(10) Add the butter and lemon and orange zest. Stir until the butter has melted.

(11) Set the filling aside to cool.

(12) When the filling is cool, brush the pastry shell with the melted butter.

(13) Pour the cooled filling into the pastry shell.

(14) Roll out the remaining pastry into a rectangle about 1/8 inch thick and at least 10 inches long.

(15) Cut the pastry with a sharp knife or a pastry wheel lengthwise into strips that are about 1/2 inch wide.

(16) Cross 2 strips over the pie at the center. Working out from the center to the edge of the pie, add the remaining strips one at a time, weaving them over and under each other in crisscross fashion. Leave about 1 inch between the strips.

(17) Trim the strips even with the bottom crust of the pie.

Moisten the edge of the bottom crust with milk for a tight seal, using the tines of a dinner fork or your fingers to press the strips tightly to the bottom crust.

(18) Bake on the bottom rack for 10 minutes then reduce heat to 350° F. and bake for about 20 minutes longer, or until the pastry is a light golden brown.

(19) Serve warm or at room temperature.

❀ INGREDIENTS

1 Double Crust Pastry (page 66)
2 1/4 cups of granulated sugar
1/4 teaspoon of ground cinnamon
1/4 cup of orange juice
2 tablespoons of water
4 cups of fresh cranberries
1 tablespoon of corn starch
2 tablespoons of cold water
2 1/2 tablespoons of butter
1 tablespoon of grated lemon zest
1 tablespoon of grated orange zest
2 tablespoons butter, melted

SERVES 6

PUMPKIN PIE

Preheat the oven to 450° F.

(1) Line a 9-inch pie plate with the pastry; prick the dough all over with a fork, flute the edge with your fingers and chill for several hours.

(2) Combine the pumpkin, sugar, salt, cinnamon, ginger, nutmeg, and cloves in a large bowl.

(3) In another large bowl, beat the eggs with a fork.

(4) Slowly add the evaporated milk to the eggs.

(5) Add the egg mixture to the pumpkin mixture and blend well.

(6) Pour the pumpkin filling into the pie shell and place in the oven.

(7) Bake on the bottom rack for 15 minutes, then reduce heat to 300° F. and bake for 45 minutes longer, or until a knife, inserted in the center, comes out clean.

(8) Cool on a wire rack.

(9) Serve slightly warm or at room temperature.

To Prepare Fresh Pumpkin: Cut the pumpkin in half; remove the seeds and stringy part. Place both sides, cut side down in a large baking dish. In an oven pre-heated to 350° F., bake for 1 hour or until tender depending on the size of the pumpkin. Scrape the pumpkin flesh off of the rind, drain; press dry between two heavy pieces of cloth, and then purée with some of the evaporated milk from the recipe.

 INGREDIENTS

1/2 Double Crust Pastry (page 66)
1 3/4 cups of cooked and puréed
  pumpkin (see note)
3/4 cup of brown sugar, firmly
  packed
1/2 teaspoon of salt
1 teaspoon of ground cin-
  namon
1/2 teaspoon of
  ground ginger
1/2 teaspoon of
  ground nutmeg
1/8 teaspoon of
  ground cloves
2 eggs
1 cup of evapo-
  rated milk

SERVES 6-8

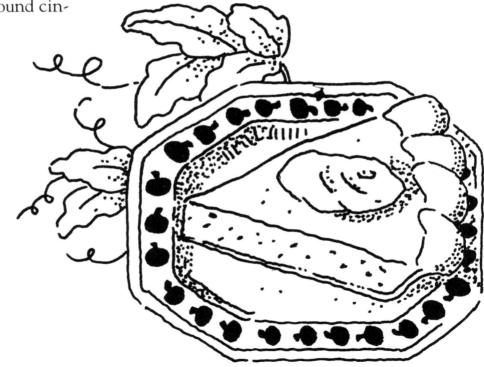

APPLE PIE - BASIC RECIPE

Preheat the oven to 425° F.

(1) Line a 9-inch pie plate with half of the pastry; prick the dough all over with a fork. Chill.

(2) Form a ball with the other half of the pastry and chill.

(3) Wash, pare, core, quarter, and slice the apples.

(4) Place 1/2 of the apples in the pastry-lined pie plate, with the sharp edges of the apples turned inward so they will not cut the pastry.

(5) Drizzle 1/2 of the lemon juice over the apples.

(6) Combine the sugar, nutmeg, and cinnamon.

(7) Sprinkle 1/2 of the sugar mixture over the apples.

(8) Top with the rest of the apples then sprinkle with the remaining sugar mixture. (Heap the apples toward the center of the pie — they cook down.)

(9) Trim the bottom pastry even with the plate rim, using scissors or a knife. Dot butter over the apples, then moisten the rim of the bottom pastry with cold water.

(10) Roll out the rest of the chilled pastry to a size a little larger than the pie plate.

(11) Cut at least 2 vents in this pastry.

(12) Place pastry on top of the apples, cut away any excess, and seal by dampening the bottom edge with cold water. Flute the edge with your fingers.

(13) Bake on the bottom rack for 40 minutes, or until the apples are tender when pricked with a toothpick, or fork.

(14) Set on a wire rack to cool.

(15) Serve warm with whipped or ice cream.

Sugar Topped Apple Pie: For a sugary upper crust, brush the top of the pie with milk, then sprinkle with 2 tablespoons of granulated sugar. Bake as above.

✸ INGREDIENTS

1 Double Crust Pastry (page 66)
4 cups of tart apples
2 teaspoons of lemon juice
2/3 cup of granulated sugar
1/2 teaspoon of ground nutmeg
1 teaspoon of ground cinnamon
1 tablespoon of butter

SERVES 6-8

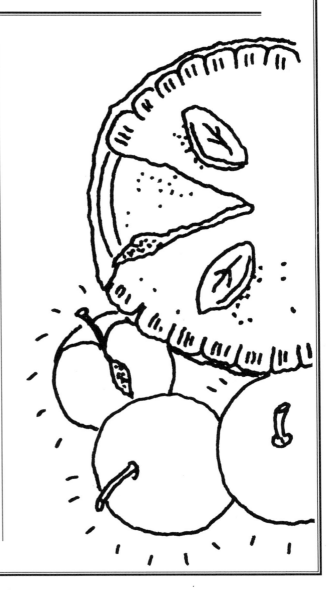

APPLE CRUMB PIE

Preheat oven to 375° F.

To Make the fruit filling:

(1) Wash, pare, core, and slice the apples.

(2) Mix together the apples, sugar, cinnamon, and vanilla extract.

(3) Arrange this mixture in a buttered 9-inch pie plate.

To Make Topping:

(1) Combine the brown sugar, butter, flour, oats, and cinnamon.

(2) Crumble the topping over the apples, but not on the rim of the pie plate.

(3) Bake for 35-40 minutes.

(4) Serve in wedges with whipped or ice cream.

❀ INGREDIENTS

Fruit Filling:
6 cups of tart apples
1 cup of sugar
1 1/2 teaspoons of ground cinnamon
1 tablespoon of vanilla extract

Topping:
1 cup of brown sugar, firmly packed
1 cup of butter, melted
1 1/2 cups of all-purpose flour
1 1/4 cups of rolled oats
1 teaspoon of ground cinnamon

SERVES 6

DEEP-DISH APPLE PIE

Preheat oven to 450° F.

(1) Roll out the pastry and cut at least 2 vents.
(2) Place on a piece of waxed paper and cover with another sheet of waxed paper; chill.
(3) Mix together the brown sugar, flour, cinnamon, salt, and nutmeg.
(4) Cut in the butter and the orange zest with a pastry blender or 2 knives until the mixture resembles coarse crumbs. Set aside.
(5) Put the apples into a large bowl and sprinkle the orange and lemon juices over them.
(6) Gently turn the apples with a fork to coat them with the juice mixture.
(7) Arrange 1/2 of the apple slices in a buttered 1 1/2- quart baking dish.
(8) Sprinkle with 1/2 of the sugar mixture.
(9) Sprinkle with 1/2 of the grated cheese; repeat from step 7 using the remaining ingredients.
(10) Top with the pastry.

❈ INGREDIENTS

1 Double Crust Pastry (page 66)
3/4 cup of brown sugar, firmly packed
3 tablespoons of flour
1 teaspoon of ground cinnamon
1/2 teaspoon of salt
1/4 teaspoon of ground nutmeg
3 tablespoons of butter
1 teaspoon of grated orange zest
6 cups of pared, cored, and thinly sliced tart apples
1/4 cup of orange juice
1 tablespoon of lemon juice
1/2 cup of grated sharp cheddar cheese

(11) Bake on the bottom rack for 10 minutes then reduce the heat to 350° F. and bake for 25- 30 minutes longer, or until the apples are tender and the crust is a light golden brown.

SERVES 6

APPLE-MINCE CRUMB PIE

Preheat oven to 425° F.

(1) Line a 9-inch pie plate with the pastry; prick the dough all over with a fork, flute the edge with your fingers and chill.
(2) Blend the apples with the mincemeat.
(3) Pour mincemeat mixture into pie shell.
(4) Prepare the crumb crust topping by blending together the brown sugar, flour, oats, cinnamon, and butter.
(5) Crumble the topping over the mincemeat mixture.
(6) Bake on the bottom rack for 30-35 minutes, or until the apples are tender.

❋ INGREDIENTS

1/2 Double Crust Pastry (page 66)
1 1/2 cups of pared, cored, and coarsely chopped tart apples
2 cups of prepared mincemeat
1/2 cup of brown sugar, firmly packed
3/4 cup of all-purpose flour
3/4 cup of rolled oats
3/4 teaspoon of ground cinnamon
1/2 cup of butter, melted

NOTE: *See recipe on page 78 for Home Style Mincemeat or purchase in your local supermarket.*

SERVES 6

MINCE PIE

Preheat the oven to 450° F.

(1) Line a 9-inch pie plate with 1/2 of the Double Crust Pastry; prick the dough all over with a fork, flute the edge with your fingers and chill.

(2) In a bowl, mix the mincemeat with the chopped apple and the brandy.

(3) Fill the pie shell with the mincemeat mixture.

(4) Roll out the remaining chilled pastry to a size a little larger than the pie plate.

(5) Cut at least 2 vents in this pastry.

(6) Place pastry on top of the mincemeat mixture, cut away any excess, and seal by dampening the bottom edge with cold water and pressing the edges together with a fork.

(7) Moisten the top crust with water or milk to facilitate browning.

(8) Bake on the bottom rack for 10 minutes, then reduce heat to 350° F. and bake about 30 minutes more, or until the crust is a golden brown. Serve warm or cool.

❂ INGREDIENTS

1 Double Crust Pastry, chilled (page 66)
3 1/2 cups of prepared mincemeat
1 apple, pared, and chopped
3 tablespoons of brandy

NOTE: *See recipe on page 78 for Home Style Mincemeat or purchase in your local supermarket.*

SERVES 6

MINCEMEAT, HOME-STYLE

(1) Place the suet, apples, brown sugar, cider, jelly, raisins, currants, molasses, salt, cinnamon, cloves, nutmeg, and mace in a large saucepan and mix thoroughly.

(2) Simmer uncovered for about 1 hour, or until most of the liquid is absorbed, stirring occasionally.

(3) Add the meat, lemon zest, and lemon juice; blend thoroughly.

(4) Set aside in covered jars in a cool place to mature for several days before using.

✸ INGREDIENTS

1 cup of ground suet
2 cups of chopped apples
2 cups of brown sugar, firmly packed
2 cups of apple cider
1/2 cup of grape jelly
2 cups of chopped seedless raisins
1 cup of currants
1/2 cup of molasses
1 teaspoon of salt
1 teaspoon of ground cinnamon
1/2 teaspoon of ground cloves
1/2 teaspoon of ground nutmeg
1/8 teaspoon of mace
2 cups of cooked ground beef
2 tablespoons of grated lemon zest
2 tablespoons of lemon juice

MAKES 3 1/2 CUPS

FRESH APPLE CAKE

Preheat oven to 350° F.

(1) Butter and flour an 8x8x2-inch cake pan. Tap excess flour free.
(2) Coarsely chop the pecans and set them aside.
(3) Sift together the flour, baking soda, cinnamon, cloves, and salt; set aside.
(4) In a bowl, cream together the butter and sugar.
(5) Gradually add the egg, beating until fluffy after each addition.
(6) Add the nuts to the dry ingredients then add this in thirds to the creamed mixture, beating until just blended after each addition (do not overbeat).
(7) Stir the apples into the mixture.
(8) Turn the mixture into the prepared pan.
(9) Bake for 45 minutes, or until a cake tester inserted into the middle of the cake tests done.
(10) Cool on a wire rack before removing cake from the pan.

❀ INGREDIENTS

1 cup of coarsely chopped pecans
1 cup of sifted flour
1 teaspoon of baking soda
1/2 teaspoon of ground cinnamon
1/4 teaspoon of ground cloves
1/4 teaspoon of salt
1/4 cup of butter
1 cup of sugar
1 egg, well beaten
2 cups of chopped apples

SERVES 8

CRANBERRY APPLESAUCE CAKE WITH ALMOND CARAMEL FROSTING

Preheat oven to 350° F.

To Make Cake:

(1) Butter and flour a 9x9x2-inch cake pan, tapping out excess flour.
(2) Sift together the flour, baking soda, cinnamon, and salt; set aside.
(3) In a large bowl, cream the butter until softened, and add the brown sugar gradually, beating until fluffy after each addition.
(4) Add the eggs in thirds, beating thoroughly after each addition.
(5) Gradually add the sifted dry ingredients.
(6) In a small bowl, blend together the applesauce, evaporated milk, and cider vinegar.
(7) Gradually add the applesauce mixture to the butter mixture, mixing until just smooth.
(8) Stir in the cranberries.
(9) Turn the batter into the prepared pan.
(10) Bake for 40 minutes, or until the cake tests done with a cake tester inserted into the middle of the cake.
(11) Place on a cooling rack while preparing the frosting.

To Make Almond Caramel Frosting:

(1) In a small bowl, cream the butter and sugar until fluffy.
(2) Add the evaporated milk and continue beating.
(3) Stir in the chopped nuts.
(4) Spread the frosting lightly over the cake.
(5) Place the cake in the broiler with the top of the cake about 4 inches from the source of the heat.
(6) Broil approximately 1 minute, or until the frosting bubbles. Watch closely to avoid scorching.

NOTE: For those who do not like nuts, almost any recipe calling for them can be successfully created without including them; nuts just add texture and a bit of flavor.

INGREDIENTS

Cake:

2 cups of flour
1 teaspoon of baking soda
1 teaspoon of ground cinnamon
1/2 teaspoon of salt
1/2 cup of butter
1 cup of packed brown sugar
2 eggs, well beaten
1 cup of thick, sweetened
  applesauce
2/3 cup of evaporated milk
1 tablespoon of cider vinegar
3/4 cup of dried cranberries

Almond Caramel Frosting

4 tablespoons of butter
1/2 cup of packed brown sugar
2 tablespoons of evaporated
  milk
1/2 cup of toasted, coarsely
  chopped almonds

SERVES 8

TURKEY PIE

Preheat the broiler

(1) Reheat the mashed potatoes.
(2) Mix the bacon into the mashed potatoes.
(3) Spread the mashed potatoes in a buttered 9x13-inch baking dish.
(4) Cover with the sliced turkey.
(5) Add the carrots, peas, and creamed onions to the gravy; mix well.
(6) Pour the gravy mixture over the turkey.
(7) Broil until golden brown, for approximately 10 minutes.
(8) Serve at once with cranberry sauce.

✸ INGREDIENTS

3 cups of leftover mashed potatoes
2/3 cup of cooked, and crumbled bacon
leftover turkey slices
1 cup of sliced carrots, cooked
1 cup of cooked peas
1 cup of leftover coarsely chopped creamed onions
1 1/2 cups of leftover gravy
2 cups of leftover cranberry sauce

NOTE: *Three cups of leftover stuffing may be substituted for the mashed potatoes and bacon.*

SERVES 6

TURKEY AND CORN PUDDING

Preheat oven to 325° F.

(1) Process the corn in a food processor.
(2) In a medium bowl, mix the flour, mustard, and butter into a paste.
(3) Add the corn, eggs, milk, onion, garlic, salt, and pepper. Mix well.
(4) Place the turkey in a greased baking dish.
(5) Pour the corn mixture over the turkey.
(6) Set in a pan containing enough hot water to come half way up the baking dish containing the pudding.
(7) Bake for 1 hour and 15 minutes, or until a knife inserted into the center of the mixture comes out clean.

❀ INGREDIENTS

1 2/3 cups of whole kernel corn
2 tablespoons of flour
1/4 teaspoon of dry mustard
2 tablespoons butter, melted
3 eggs, beaten
3 cups of milk
1/4 cup of minced onion
1 clove of garlic, minced
salt and pepper to taste
2 cups of diced leftover turkey

SERVES 6-8

TURKEY ROYALE

Preheat oven to 375° F.

(1) Combine milk and 1 tablespoon of butter in a double boiler. Heat until the butter has melted.
(2) Beat the egg yolks in a small bowl.
(3) Pour a small amount of the hot milk mixture into the egg yolks and blend.
(4) Gradually add the egg yolks into the milk mixture whisking after each addition.
(5) In a small skillet, sauté the mushrooms and garlic in the remaining 2 tablespoons of butter for 5 minutes.
(6) Sprinkle the mushrooms with flour and whisk into the hot milk.
(7) Add the red pepper, turkey, bread crumbs, thyme, parsley, salt, and pepper.
(8) Beat the egg whites until they form moist, not dry, peaks.
(9) Fold in the egg whites, then pour into a buttered 1 1/2-quart baking dish.
(10) Set in a pan containing enough hot water to come half-way up the

❀ INGREDIENTS

3/4 cup of warm milk
3 tablespoons of butter
2 eggs, separated
1 cup of sliced mushrooms
1 clove of garlic, minced
1 tablespoon of flour
1/4 cup of diced red pepper
1 1/2 cups of coarsely chopped cooked turkey
1/4 cup of soft bread crumbs
1/4 teaspoon of thyme
2 tablespoons of chopped parsley
salt and pepper to taste
1 1/2 cups of grated sharp cheddar cheese

baking dish.
(11) Bake for 30 minutes, sprinkle the cheese on top and return to the oven.
(12) Bake for 10 more minutes or until the cheese is bubbling and lightly browned on top.

SERVES 4

TURKEY SANDWICHES

(1) Spread the cranberry sauce on
    1 slice of toast.
(2) Layer the turkey, bacon, tomatoes,
    stuffing, and lettuce on top.
(3) Spread mayonnaise on the
    remaining slice of toast.
(4) Place toast on top of the sandwich
    and cut in half.

❀ INGREDIENTS

2 slices of bread, toasted
1 tablespoon of cranberry sauce
2 slices of leftover turkey
2 slices of bacon, cooked
2 slices of tomatoes
1/4 cup of leftover stuffing
2 lettuce leaves
1 tablespoon of mayonnaise

NOTE: *Serve these sandwiches at
the end of a busy Thanksgiving
day.*

MAKES 1 SANDWICH

TURKEY SALAD

(1) Place the turkey and eggs in
  a bowl.
(2) Add the mayonnaise, onion, celery,
  lemon juice, salt and pepper and
  blend well; chill.
(3) Serve on lettuce leaves or on toast.

❁ INGREDIENTS

2 cups of diced leftover turkey
2 hard boiled eggs, chopped
3-4 heaping tablespoons of
  mayonnaise
1/4 cup of minced onion
1/4 cup of minced celery
1 tablespoon of lemon juice
salt and pepper to taste

SERVES 2

TURKEY HASH

(1) Place turkey into a large bowl.
(2) Add the potatoes, stuffing, and onion to the turkey.
(3) Add the leftover turkey gravy, salt and pepper to taste. Blend the mixture well (it should be crumbly).
(4) Heat the oil in a large skillet and add the hash.
(5) Form the hash into a large patty with a spatula.
(6) Cook until browned and crusty on the bottom.
(7) Turn and brown the other side (it doesn't matter if it crumbles; simply reshape it).
(8) Meanwhile, poach the eggs.
(9) To serve, divide the hash into 4 equal portions and top each portion with a poached egg.
(10) Serve with cranberry sauce.

❀ INGREDIENTS

3 cups of coarsely chopped leftover turkey
1 cup of finely diced leftover boiled potatoes
2 cups of leftover stuffing
1/4 cup of minced onion
1 cup of leftover turkey gravy
salt and pepper to taste
3 tablespoons of oil
4 eggs
1 1/2 cups of cranberry sauce

SERVES 4

INDEX

Traditional Country Life Recipe Books from
BRICK TOWER PRESS

American Chef's Companion
Chocolate Companion
Apple Companion
Fresh Herb Companion
Pumpkin Companion
Victorian Christmas Cookery

Forthcoming Titles
Fresh Bread Companion
Soups, Stews, Chowders

MAIL ORDER AND GENERAL INFORMATION

Many of our titles are carried by your local book store, gift, or museum shop.

If they do not already carry our line please ask them to write us for information.

If you are unable to purchase our titles from your local shop, call or write to us.

Our titles are available through mail order. Just send a check or money order for $9.95 per title with $1.50 postage to the address below or call us Monday through Friday, 9 AM to 5 PM, EST. We accept Visa and Mastercard.

Send all mail order, book club, catalog and special sales requests to the address below or call us. We would like to hear from you.

Brick Tower Press
1230 Park Avenue, 10th Floor
New York, NY 10128 US

Telephone & Facsimile
1-212-427-7139, 1-800-68-BRICK, bricktower@aol.com